Short Stack Editions | Volume 28

Cucumbers

by Dawn Perry

Short Stack Editions

Publisher: Nick Fauchald
Creative Director: Rotem Raffe
Editor: Kaitlyn Goalen
Copy Editor: Abby Tannenbaum
Marketing Manager: Erin Fritch

Distributed in the United States by Dovetail Press (dovetail.press).

ISBN 978-0-9975321-8-0

Printed in Virginia
June 2017

Table of Contents

Cold

Condiments & More

Sweets

In the process of editing our Short Stack series, we've started mentally placing most recipes into two major groups: the "bookmark" group and the "make this now" group. The former is full of recipes that make our mouths water with an anticipatory longing. They are a pleasure to read, and we flag them for a future afternoon when we find ourselves with a few extra hours to kill.

But the reality of our daily cooking routine (and probably yours) requires something simpler. We're talking about the "make this now" category, which mostly includes recipes that have short prep times and reasonable ingredient lists, but are still delicious and satisfying.

Somehow Dawn Perry has assembled an entire book of "make this now" food. Each of her recipes gets you the greatest amount of flavor in the least amount of moves, like some kind of kitchen jujitsu. The result: We cook these recipes on a weekly basis.

Appropriately, the style of these recipes perfectly suits the ingredient they celebrate: cucumbers. While cukes, like all produce, have a season—the peak of summer brings a bounty of sizes and colors and flavors—they are a year-round constant in our crisper drawer. In an era where cookbook recipes (including some of ours) are often weighed down with steps, this edition feels downright refreshing—just like the cucumber itself.

So get going. Make these now.

—*The Editors*

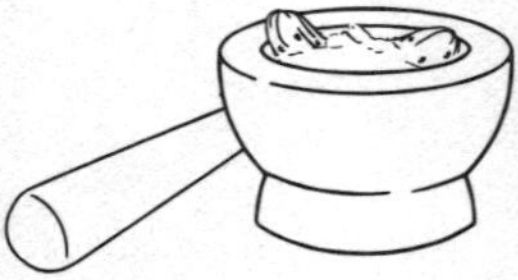

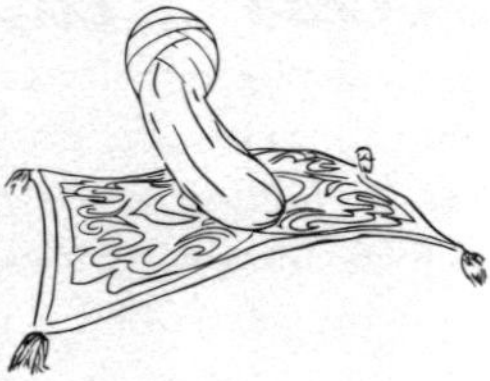

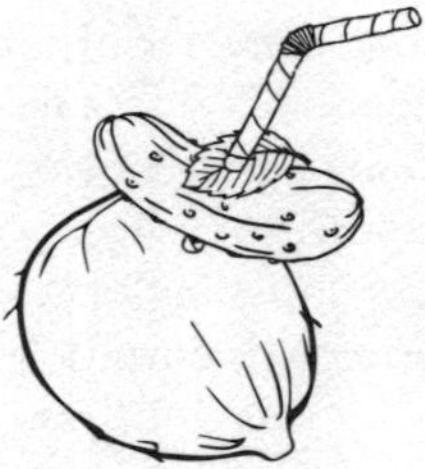

Introduction

I was kind of a picky eater as a kid. "Just one more bite," my mom would plead, generally over vegetables, particularly green beans. But the one preparation we never battled over was her cucumber salad. It was nothing more than sliced cucumbers, chopped red onion, dill, vinegar, salt and pepper. It was simple, refreshing and came together in about three minutes. My mouth puckers just thinking about it. I wouldn't call the bulk of my childhood diet "light," but that bracing cucumber salad was a welcome palate cleanser for whatever came before or after.

When I was growing up, cucumbers would show up at our house from all sides during the summer: from our next-door neighbors, gifted gardeners Norman and Dotty, or from "Coach" across the street. They'd also show up with my grandfather, who grew them in a tiny rectangular plot behind his house. We ate a lot of cucumber salad.

Luckily, these days you can find pretty great cucumbers in the supermarket year-round. I tend to buy English and Persian varieties because I prefer their sweeter flesh and thin skins and I don't need to peel or seed them. But if you hit the farmers' market in late July and early August, you'll see all kinds of cukes laid out in bushels: Kirbys for pickling, Blonde or lemon cucumbers for slicing, sweet Armenians and, my personal favorite, the Diva cucumber. Although they all look a little different, they taste largely the same and can be used almost interchangeably in the recipes that follow.

When I started this project, I was aware of some of cucumbers' potential, but I didn't realize half of what they would reveal to me through the process. Sure, I knew they could be pickled with different vinegars, herbs or spices, and obviously they can be a fresh addition to salads. But they also love to be cooked over smoldering coals, in a screaming hot pan, and even baked with butter, which produces something at once crisp and tender.

In Eastern medicine, cucumbers are prized for their cooling properties; they're thought to clear toxins, improve digestion and quench thirst. Their mellowing nature balances big assertive flavors and contrasting textures like Indian spices, salty feta and hot chiles. It's no wonder cucumbers are at their prime during the hottest months of the year. They're so naturally refreshing, in fact, that they can even brighten up a bottle of gin when they're left to soak inside for a few days.

In addition, cucumbers can grow just about anywhere. I once saw a cucumber growing through the holes of a chain link fence in the yard of a public school in Harlem. I was at the elementary school with some coworkers to paint benches in the garden as part of their indoor-outdoor kitchen classroom. The bulk of the produce stayed tethered to where the students had planted it, growing in neat, easy-to-harvest rows. But not this cucumber. This one rose up clear out of the garden, wove itself in and out of the fence's links and sprouted an impressive fruit like a baseball bat pointing confidently toward the outfield. It seemed to whisper, "Watch what I can do."

—Dawn Perry

Recipes

Know Your Cukes

Cucumbers are largely divided into two categories: those for pickling and those for slicing. Kirbys and gherkins are generally used for pickling, but a greater variety of slicers seem to pop up every summer. If you're lucky, you might find Dashers and Divas, Blondes or Mexican Sour Gherkins (those are the ones that look like mini watermelons). If you can't find any of the rarer breeds, one of these more common varieties should keep you as cool as, well, you know.

Slicing cucumbers are best for, duh, slicing and eating raw. These medium-size (about eight ounces) dark-green cukes are usually found in your local grocery store. Sometimes their skins are waxed to prolong shelf life, so it's best to peel the ones you buy at the supermarket. Their seeds can be bitter and, at the very least, distracting. To remove them, halve the cucumber lengthwise and use a teaspoon to scrape the seeds out, then slice or chop and add to snack bags or salads.

Kirby cucumbers are short and squat with bumpy skin that usually fades from dark to light green from one end to the other. They have thin skins and slightly drier flesh, which is ideal for soaking up the flavors of a pickle brine. Kirbys can vary in size, but there are about four in a pound.

English or hothouse cucumbers have vibrant green skin and are about a foot long and roughly 12 ounces each. They are typically sold sealed in plastic and are sometimes labeled "seedless" because their tiny seeds are few and far between. Thin skins and crunchy texture make them perfect for tossing into hassle-free weeknight salads, and their slightly sweet flesh is delicious blended into a refreshing green juice.

Persian cucumbers look a little like a baby version of the English variety. Because they're extra crunchy, they go nicely with anything rich and creamy, like meat, mozzarella or cream cheese. At about an inch in diameter and six inches long, they make the prettiest crudité when they're quartered lengthwise.

Lemon cucumbers are short and round and look just like their namesake. They have thin skins and mild flesh, and are great for slicing, snacking and practical jokes. About the size of tennis balls, they're easy to pack inside a wide-mouth pickling jar, too.

Armenian cucumbers aren't actually cucumbers at all but a type of muskmelon (you might notice their cantaloupe-like fragrance when they're sliced). You'll mostly find these fluted beauties at the farmers' market. Look for long, curving shapes with pale-green skin. They can grow large—up to two feet long—but they get bitter when they're too mature, so pick ones that are closer to 12 inches in length and two inches in diameter and use them for slicing or pickling.

Spicy Garlic Dill Pickles

These days, it's easy to find just about everything, from beets to Brussels sprouts, pickled. But in my kitchen (and most, I'd argue), cucumbers are still king. Their thin skins, crisp mild flesh and edible seeds make them ideal for soaking up a range of flavored brines. These are quick pickles, intended to be eaten within a couple of weeks rather than stored on a shelf in the basement. This recipe is based on my grandmother Gogs's recipe. I like its simplicity: It doesn't require heat or special ingredients—just a bit of patience (but only a day). Dill is a safe bet, but I've made these with fresh oregano and basil, too. And while I'll encourage you to riff to your heart's content (try different vinegars, for instance), don't go crazy with the sugar; save the sweetness for the Bread & Butter Pickles (page 13).

¾ cup apple cider vinegar

4 garlic cloves, smashed and roughly chopped

1 chile de arbol, lightly crushed, or 1 teaspoon red pepper flakes (optional)

1 tablespoon kosher salt

2 teaspoons black peppercorns, lightly crushed

1 teaspoon sugar

1 pound Kirby cucumbers (about 4), halved lengthwise

Several dill sprigs

makes 1 quart

In a quart-size glass jar, combine the vinegar, garlic, chile (if using), salt, peppercorns and sugar. Close the jar tightly and shake until the salt and sugar dissolve.

Add the cucumbers and dill to the jar, then add enough cold water to cover the cucumbers. Close tightly and shake to combine. Refrigerate for at least 24 hours before serving. The pickles will keep, covered, in the refrigerator for up to 3 weeks.

Bread & Butter Pickles

If you think you don't like sweet pickles (like me), give these a try. The distilled vinegar offers enough sharpness to offset the sweetness of the sugar, while shallot, bay leaf and celery seed keep things leaning just savory enough. Use these on burgers, hot dogs or, my personal favorite, fried chicken sandwiches.

- 1 cup distilled white vinegar
- ½ cup sugar
- 1 tablespoon kosher salt
- 1 teaspoon celery seeds
- 1 shallot, thinly sliced into rings
- 2 fresh or dried bay leaves
- 1 pound Kirby cucumbers (about 4), sliced crosswise into ¼- to ½-inch rounds

makes 1 quart

In a small saucepan, combine the vinegar, sugar, salt, celery seeds, shallot and bay leaves. Bring to a boil and cook, stirring often, until the sugar has dissolved, about 4 minutes. Remove the pan from the heat.

Place the cucumbers in a quart-size glass jar. Pour the vinegar mixture over the top and add enough cold water (about 1 cup) just to cover. Close the jar tightly and shake to combine. Refrigerate for at least 24 hours before serving. The pickles will keep, covered, in the refrigerator for up to 3 weeks.

Indian-Spiced Cucumbers

These fall somewhere between a pickle and a relish, but if you prefer to eat your cukes in spear form, go ahead and cut them into long, thin pieces or however you like. Whatever shape they're in, put them out whenever you have Indian flavors elsewhere in your meal, or make an instant vinaigrette by tossing them with some greens and a drizzle of olive oil. For a special treat, wrap them in a piece of warm naan with grilled merguez and a dollop of thick yogurt.

2 teaspoons cumin seeds, lightly crushed

1 teaspoon coriander seeds, lightly crushed

1 teaspoon fennel seeds, lightly crushed

1 teaspoon fenugreek, lightly crushed

1 teaspoon mustard seeds

½ to 1 teaspoon red pepper flakes, depending on your heat preference

1 cup distilled white vinegar

1 tablespoon light brown sugar

1 tablespoon kosher salt

3 garlic cloves, finely chopped

1 ounce ginger, thinly sliced

½ teaspoon ground turmeric

1 pound Kirby cucumbers (about 4), cut into ½-inch dice

makes 1 quart

In a small saucepan over medium-high heat, combine the cumin, coriander, fennel, fenugreek, mustard and red pepper flakes. Cook, swirling often, until the spices are fragrant and start to darken slightly, 1 to 2 minutes. Immediately add the vinegar, sugar, salt, garlic, ginger and turmeric and bring to a boil. Cook, stirring occasionally, until the sugar and salt have dissolved, about 3 minutes. Remove the pan from the heat.

Place the cucumbers in a quart-size glass jar. Pour the vinegar mixture over the top and add enough cold water (about 1 cup) just to cover. Close the jar tightly and shake to combine. Refrigerate for at least 24 hours before serving. The cukes will keep, covered, in the refrigerator for up to 3 weeks.

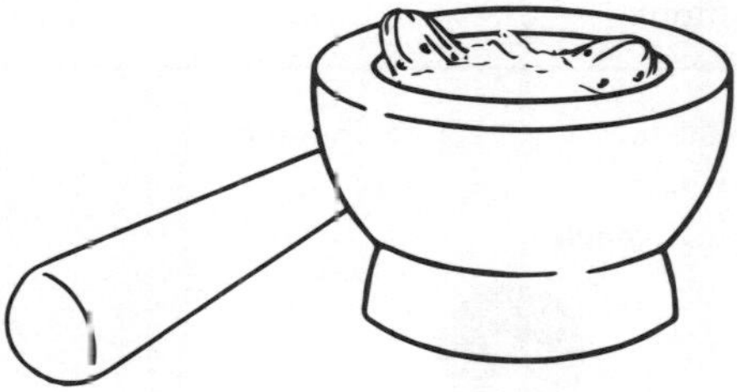

Growing Cucumbers

Even if you have limited growing space (like a fire escape), you can grow cucumbers, as long as the area gets plenty of sun and you commit to watering. Because many varieties are "vining," you can train them to grow up—and not out—to save space. Simply work the vines in and out of a trellis, tomato cage, or a fence with a few nails in it as they get taller.

Cucumber, Mint & Coconut Cooler

Cucumbers are comprised of 96 percent water. When you blend them with mint, a little lemon and super-hydrating coconut water, you've got the ultimate hot-weather refresher. You can use fresh basil or even arugula (for a spicier version) in place of the mint. Drink this first thing in the morning, and you'll feel like you've been watered like a plant.

1 large English cucumber, peeled and roughly chopped

1 cup mint leaves, plus a couple sprigs for serving

1 cup coconut water

Juice of 1 lemon

serves 2

In a blender, combine all the ingredients and process until very smooth. Strain the mixture through a fine-mesh sieve set over a pitcher, pressing on the solids to extract as much juice as possible. Pour the cooler into ice-filled glasses, garnish with mint sprigs and serve.

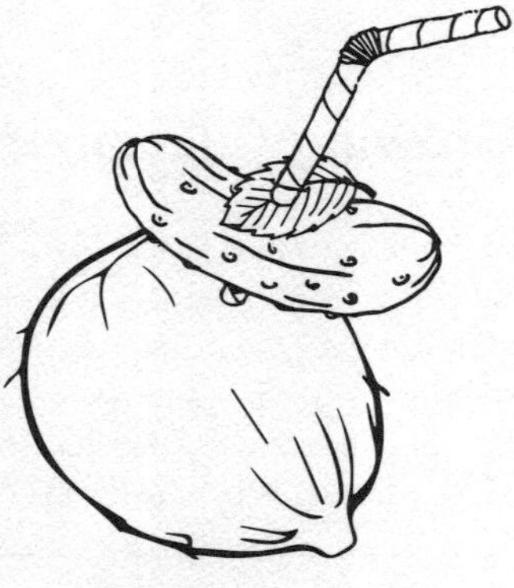

Cucumber-Celery Agua Fresca

I first tried agua fresca when I was living in San Francisco right after college. I was doing an AmeriCorps program and living on a meager stipend (so meager that I qualified for food stamps, but that's another story). Every Friday, our "Youth In Action" crew would head out for veggie burritos and aguas frescas near our office in the Mission District. Each week, I chose a new flavor: watermelon, cantaloupe, hibiscus or sometimes cucumber. Serve this drink with tacos, burritos and other spicy stuff. It also works nicely as a tequila chaser.

2 large seedless cucumbers

4 celery stalks

½ cup fresh lime juice, plus lime slices for serving

¼ cup sugar

serves 4

In a blender, combine all the ingredients with 2 cups of water and process until very smooth, about 1 minute. Strain the mixture through a fine-mesh sieve set over a pitcher and chill until ready to serve, at least 1 hour or overnight. Pour into ice-filled glasses, garnish with lime slices and serve, preferably with a straw.

Cucumber-Fennel Limeade

If it didn't make me feel like a child, I would order lemonade at every meal. I designed this recipe so I can enjoy my favorite beverage without shame. The fennel and cucumber keep this on the slightly savory side, while lime juice in place of lemon highlights the cucumber's color and sweetness. Don't discard those cucumber skins: Add them to the fennel syrup to impart another layer of cucumber flavor to the base. To make an adult soda, finish the drink with seltzer instead of still water.

- ½ cup sugar
- 1 tablespoon fennel seeds, lightly crushed
- 1 English cucumber, peeled and roughly chopped, peels reserved
- ½ cup fresh lime juice, divided

serves 4

In a small saucepan, combine the sugar, fennel seeds and ⅓ cup of water. Bring the mixture to a simmer and cook, swirling occasionally, until the sugar has dissolved, about 3 minutes. Add the cucumber peels and let cool.

In a blender, puree the cucumber with ¼ cup of lime juice until smooth. Set a fine-mesh sieve over a large pitcher and strain the cucumber mixture; discard the solids.

Place the sieve over the pitcher again, and strain the fennel syrup into the cucumber mixture, discarding the solids. Add the remaining ¼ cup of lime juice and 1½ cups of water to the pitcher and stir to combine. Serve the limeade in glasses over ice.

Cucumber-Infused Gin & Tonic

Keep in mind that every gin has its own unique balance of juniper and botanicals. Plymouth is my favorite brand because it's silky smooth, kind of grassy and really sings with the addition of cucumber (Beefeater is another fine choice). I don't particularly like highballs—they go down too quickly—so I serve this one in a rocks glass. Whatever you do, be sure to use plenty of ice and a fresh bottle of bubbles: tonic to make a G&T, or club soda for a gin rickey.

- 1 cup gin (I like Plymouth)
- 1 cup sliced Persian cucumbers (1 to 2 cucumbers, depending on the size)
- Tonic or club soda
- Lime wedges, for serving

makes -4-

In a resealable container (preferably a glass one), combine the gin and cucumber and shake to combine. Set aside in a cool dark place for 5 to 7 days, shaking the jar gently when you remember to. Using a fine-mesh sieve, strain the mixture into another glass container and discard the cucumbers.

Place 2 ounces (¼ cup) of the gin in a rocks glass and fill the glass with ice. Top with tonic or club soda and squeeze a big lime wedge over the top. Repeat to make 3 more drinks and serve.

Soy & Wasabi-Glazed Cucumbers with Crab & Lemon

When it comes to cooking cucumbers, high heat is paramount, whether it's in a skillet, on a grill or under the broiler. That way, you get some nice color and flavor on the exterior while still maintaining that precious refreshing crunch. The key to crispy crab and blistered cucumbers in this dish is no touching. Get your skillet nice and hot before you add anything, then sear without touching, stir briefly, repeat.

2 tablespoons neutral oil (such as vegetable), divided

8 ounces lump crabmeat, picked over for shell fragments

1 pound Persian cucumbers (about 6), sliced

Kosher salt

1 tablespoon sugar

1 tablespoon soy sauce

1 tablespoon rice vinegar

1 teaspoon wasabi paste

2 scallions, thinly sliced

Steamed rice, for serving

Lemon wedges, for serving

serves · 4 ·

In a large skillet over medium-high heat, add 1 tablespoon of oil. When it shimmers, add the crab and cook, tossing occasionally, until very crispy in spots, about 4 minutes; transfer to a plate.

Add the remaining tablespoon of oil to the skillet. When it shimmers, add the cucumbers and season with salt. Cook, tossing occasionally, until blistered in spots, about 4 minutes.

Meanwhile, in a small bowl, whisk together the sugar, soy sauce, vinegar and wasabi paste until the sugar has dissolved. Add the liquid mixture and the crab to the skillet and cook, tossing, until the liquid is reduced and coats the cucumbers, 1 to 2 minutes. Add the scallions and toss. Serve the cucumbers and crab over rice with a squeeze of lemon.

Storing Cucumbers

Store cucumbers in a resealable plastic bag or other container in the refrigerator. They should keep for about a week as long as you keep them dry, but eat them sooner than later: once they start to soften, it's too late.

Spicy Cucumbers & Beef with Black Vinegar, Garlic & Herbs

Cooked cucumbers are relatively new to me. I grew up largely on vinegary salads of sharp red onion and sliced raw cucumbers, but adding heat unleashes a sexier side I never knew cucumbers had. Here, when they're cooked in rendered beef fat and showered with herbs, the cucumbers end up rich and unctuous. Don't tell the other recipes in this Stack, but I think this one might be my favorite.

2 medium cucumbers (about 12 ounces), halved lengthwise

2 tablespoons neutral oil (such as vegetable)

4 garlic cloves, finely chopped

2 long red chiles (such as finger or red serrano), finely chopped

1 pound ground beef

Kosher salt

1 medium shallot, thinly sliced

2 tablespoons black vinegar (available at Asian markets)

1 tablespoon soy sauce

1 teaspoon sugar

Freshly ground black pepper

Steamed rice, cooked ramen noodles or chopped romaine, for serving

Handful of mint leaves (about ½ cup)

Handful of basil leaves (about ½ cup)

Handful of cilantro leaves and tender stems (about ½ cup)

serves –4–

Cut the cucumbers into 4-inch lengths. Place them cut side down on a cutting board. Using the side of a large knife, crush the cucumbers by pressing down on them until you feel them give way (similar to when you pit an olive), then slice crosswise into ½-inch-thick pieces. Set aside.

In a large skillet, heat the oil over medium-high heat. Add the garlic and chiles and cook, stirring often, until fragrant and softened, about 2 minutes. Add the beef, season with salt and cook, breaking up the meat with a wooden spoon, until cooked through, about 5 minutes. Continue to cook, stirring occasionally, until the meat is crispy all over, 6 to 8 minutes longer.

Add the cucumbers and shallot and cook, tossing occasionally and scraping up any browned bits stuck to the bottom of the skillet, until the cucumbers are softened and translucent, about 4 minutes. Add the vinegar, soy sauce and sugar and cook, stirring, until the sauce reduces slightly, about 2 minutes; season to taste with salt and pepper.

Spoon the beef and cucumber mixture over rice, noodles or greens, top with herbs and serve on a platter or divide among individual plates.

Butter-Baked Cucumbers

Who knew cucumbers could play so nicely with butter? Apparently Julia Child did. In my research, I found some pretty fussy recipes for butter-baked cukes, including one that required cutting the cucumbers in batons, finely chopping the herbs and a bunch of other steps I promptly forgot. This is a much simpler and, I have to guess, much more delicious approach. Use Persian cucumbers for this one: Their taut flesh stays firm after baking, so they end up crisp-tender but never mushy. Serve them alongside seared or steamed fish filets or sautéed shrimp.

- 1 pound Persian cucumbers (about 6), halved lengthwise
- 1 small shallot, thinly sliced into rings
- 3 tablespoons unsalted butter, cut into pieces
- Kosher salt and freshly ground black pepper
- Small handful tender herbs such as tarragon, dill or parsley

serves 4

Preheat the oven to 425°. In a large shallow baking dish, arrange the cucumbers cut side up. Top with the shallot and butter and season with salt and pepper. Transfer the dish to the oven and roast, basting the cucumbers with the melted butter that accumulates in the dish halfway through, until the cucumbers are tender, the shallot is golden and the butter is browned, 20 to 25 minutes. Baste one more time with the butter, top with herbs and serve.

Spicy Crushed Thai Cucumbers

Once you start crushing your cucumbers, you may never go back. It's a simple trick used in Asian cooking that helps the cukes absorb dressings and marinades so every bite is an explosion of flavor. Use as much or as little Thai chile as you like depending on your heat preference. Serve these with big juicy salt and pepper steaks or as a condiment for rice bowls and noodle dishes.

1½ pounds Persian cucumbers (about 9)

1 teaspoon salt, divided

1 teaspoon sugar, divided

2 tablespoons rice vinegar

2 teaspoons fish sauce

1 shallot, thinly sliced

1 garlic clove, finely chopped or grated

1 to 2 Thai bird chiles, thinly sliced

Small handful opal basil (if you can't find opal, Italian basil is fine)

serves 4 *to* 6

Cut the ends off the cucumbers. Using the side of a large knife, press down on the cucumbers until you feel them give way (similar to when you pit an olive). Once they're crushed, slice the cucumbers crosswise into ½-inch pieces, cutting about a third of the slices in half (you'll see obvious places to cut). Place the cucumbers in a fine-mesh sieve and sprinkle with ½ teaspoon each of salt and sugar. Let the cucumbers drain into the sink for about 20 minutes (don't rinse).

In a large bowl, whisk together the vinegar, fish sauce, shallot, garlic, chiles and the remaining ½ teaspoon each of salt and sugar. Add the drained cucumbers, toss to combine and serve. You can eat them right away, but their flavors will intensify as they sit.

Cucumber Soup with a Splash of Tomato

I'm generally not a big fan of cold soup, but when you pair this creamy cucumber version with a splash of spicy hot tomato soup, it goes down mighty easy. I've called for English cucumbers here so you don't have to peel or seed them, but if you have only standard cucumbers, feel free to use them—just peel them and scoop out the seeds before blending. I like to serve the cucumber soup chilled and the tomato soup hot. Served with a spoonful of sour cream, the pairing is a perfect showcase for cucumber's cooling qualities.

For the cucumber soup:

2 English cucumbers, unpeeled and chopped

5 scallions, chopped

½ cup sour cream, plus more for serving

1 teaspoon rice vinegar

Pinch sugar

Kosher salt and freshly ground black pepper

For the tomato soup:

2 tablespoons olive oil

5 scallions, thinly sliced, dark green parts reserved

Kosher salt and freshly ground black pepper

One 14.5-ounce can cherry tomatoes, drained

¼ to ½ teaspoon cayenne pepper

serves 4

Make the cucumber soup: In a blender, combine the cucumbers, scallions, sour cream, vinegar, sugar and ¾ cup of water and puree until smooth; season with salt and pepper. Chill until ready to serve.

Make the tomato soup: In a medium saucepan over medium-high heat, add the oil. When it shimmers, add the scallions (white and light green parts) and cook, stirring often, until they're soft but haven't taken on any color, about 3 minutes; season with salt and pepper. Add the tomatoes and cayenne and cook, breaking up the tomatoes with a wooden spoon until the mixture starts to thicken, about 2 minutes. Add ½ cup of water, season with salt and pepper and bring to a simmer. Cook, stirring often, until slightly reduced, about 5 minutes. Transfer the mixture to a blender and puree until smooth. Keep warm or chill.

Divide the cucumber soup among 4 bowls, then add a splash of tomato soup, a dollop of sour cream and a sprinkle of the reserved scallion greens to each bowl and serve.

Mixed Cucumber & Cured Olive Salad with Whipped Feta

Right around mid-July, you'll see gardens and farmers' markets explode with cucumbers. First it's the Kirbys, then the Persians. Those will be great in this recipe, but if you can hold out until early August, you'll start to see all kinds of cool varieties hit the stands. If you can find lemon cucumbers, Blonde cucumbers and Diva cucumbers, use a combination of them to get a pretty medley of colors and shapes. Or just use a couple of English cucumbers. Those will be delicious, too.

1½ pounds mixed cucumbers, thinly sliced

1 teaspoon kosher salt, plus more to taste

8 ounces feta cheese

3 tablespoons sour cream or crème fraîche

4 tablespoons olive oil, divided, plus more for drizzling

Freshly ground black pepper

1 teaspoon lemon zest

Juice from 1 lemon

½ cup pitted oil-cured olives

Small handful fresh mint leaves

serves 4 to 6

In a large bowl, toss the cucumbers with 1 teaspoon of salt. Set them aside, tossing occasionally, until the cucumbers have softened slightly and released some of their liquid, about 20 minutes.

Meanwhile, in a food processor, combine the feta, sour cream and 3 tablespoons of oil and process until smooth, scraping down the sides of the bowl as needed. Taste the mixture to see if it needs salt (most feta is plenty salty on its own) and season with pepper. Transfer to a bowl and stir in the lemon zest.

Add the lemon juice and the remaining tablespoon of oil to the cucumbers and toss to combine. Season with pepper and toss again.

Spread the whipped feta on a platter and top with cucumbers (leaving the dressing behind). Add the olives and mint on top, drizzle with cucumber dressing from the bowl and a little more oil and serve.

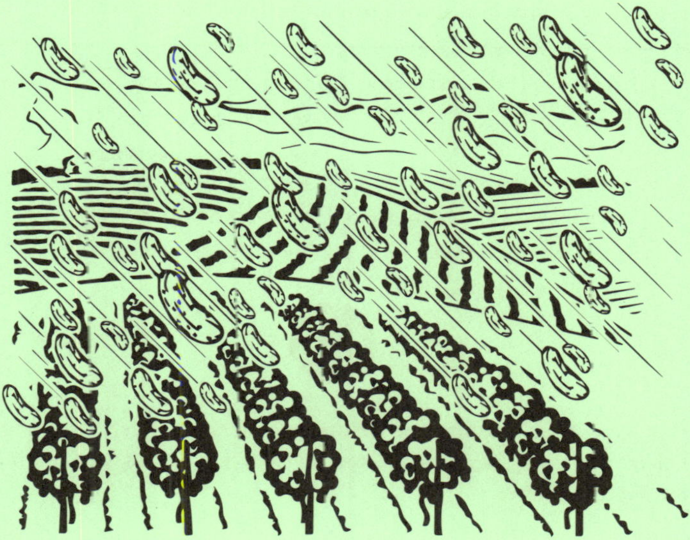

Cucumber, Tomato & Burrata Salad with Fennel Dukkha

You could easily leave the tomatoes out of this salad and bump up the cucumbers if you're feeling cucumber crazy (if you're reading this book, you probably are!). The rich creaminess of the burrata highlights the lean crunch of the cucumbers and vice versa, but if you can't find burrata, fresh mozzarella will do just fine. This is especially pretty made with ripe green heirloom tomatoes.

4 Persian or Kirby cucumbers (about ¾ to 1 pound), sliced

1 teaspoon kosher salt

1 lemon, halved

1 tablespoon black sesame seeds

1 teaspoon fennel seeds

½ teaspoon cumin seeds

½ teaspoon flaky salt

½ teaspoon red pepper flakes

3 medium tomatoes (about ½ pound), sliced

One 4-ounce ball burrata

Olive oil, for drizzling

serves 4 to 6

In a large bowl, combine the cucumbers and salt. Squeeze the lemon halves over the cucumbers and toss to combine. Set aside to marinate for 5 to 10 minutes.

Meanwhile, in a mortar and pestle, lightly crush the sesame seeds, fennel seeds and cumin seeds (alternatively, you can coarsely chop them on a cutting board). Add the flaky salt and red pepper flakes and stir to combine.

Arrange the cucumbers and tomatoes on a platter. Tear the burrata into large pieces and scatter on top of the vegetables. Drizzle with oil, sprinkle with the spice mixture and serve.

Sweet Chile Cucumbers with Chicken & Peanuts

This is my ideal summer salad: spicy, crunchy and refreshing. It's a great way to use up leftover roasted or grilled chicken or, come to think of it, Thanksgiving turkey (the spicy Asian flavors will be a relief after all that maple and sage). But why wait for leftover poultry? Just grab a rotisserie bird on the way home from work and make this tonight. English cucumbers are the way to go here, since you don't need to peel or seed them. Just chop and drop and you've got dinner.

- 1 English cucumber, halved lengthwise and thinly sliced
- 1 teaspoon kosher salt
- 1 small serrano chile, thinly sliced
- 2 tablespoons rice vinegar
- 2 teaspoons honey
- 1 teaspoon toasted sesame oil
- 2 cups cooked shredded chicken (from about 2 breasts)
- 2 celery stalks, thinly sliced
- 1 cup packed cilantro leaves
- ¼ cup salted roasted peanuts, roughly chopped

serves 2 to 4

In a large bowl, season the cucumbers with the salt. Toss the cucumbers and set aside until they release some of their liquid, about 30 minutes.

Meanwhile, combine the chile, vinegar, honey and oil in a small bowl, whisking until the honey dissolves; season with salt and pepper (but go easy—the cucumbers will be seasoned pretty well).

Drain the cucumbers and taste one. If it's too salty for you, rinse the cucumbers and drain again. In a large bowl, combine the cucumbers, chicken, celery and cilantro leaves. Add the dressing and peanuts, toss to combine and serve.

Soba Salad with Cucumbers, Soft Tofu & Quick Chile Oil

Salting cucumbers draws out excess liquid to help keep them crunchy. It also helps prevent a dreaded watery dip situation, say, in the case of tzatziki. (Pro tip for your next batch of that classic cucumber-yogurt sauce: Toss the cucumbers with salt, set them aside, then pour off the liquid after about 15 minutes before mixing them into the yogurt.) However, in this salad, rather than wasting the extracted cucumber liquid, I use it to fortify the dressing with more cucumber flavor. Once the cucumbers have released their juices, whisk the liquid into the dressing for big, fresh flavor against the cold, buttery tofu.

1 medium seedless cucumber, thinly sliced

Kosher salt

One 1-inch piece ginger, peeled and finely grated

1 garlic clove, finely chopped or grated

3 tablespoons soy sauce

3 tablespoons rice vinegar

2 teaspoons toasted sesame oil

9 ounces soba noodles

14 ounces silken tofu

Quick Chile Oil (recipe follows)

1 tablespoon black sesame seeds

Large handful torn fresh basil leaves

serves 4

Place the cucumbers in a large bowl and season with ½ teaspoon of salt. Set aside, tossing occasionally, until the cucumbers have released some of their liquid, about 15 minutes.

Drain off any accumulated juices into a separate medium bowl, and whisk in the ginger, garlic, soy sauce, vinegar and oil. Pour over the cucumbers and toss to combine.

Bring a medium pot of salted water to a boil. Add the soba noodles and cook until tender, about 4 minutes. Drain, rinse under cold water, then drain once more.

Add the drained soba noodles to the cucumber mixture and toss to combine. Divide the noodles and cucumbers among 4 bowls and top each with a spoonful of tofu. Drizzle each bowl with some of the Quick Chile Oil, sprinkle with sesame seeds and basil and serve.

Quick Chile Oil

- ¼ cup vegetable oil
- 1 teaspoon red pepper flakes
- 1 whole dried chile such as chile de arbol or Calabrian, lightly crushed

In a small saucepan over medium heat, combine the oil, red pepper flakes and dried chile. Cook, swirling occasionally, until fragrant and sizzling, about 4 minutes. Remove the pan from the heat and transfer the oil to a bowl or glass jar; let cool (no need to strain the chile). The oil will keep, tightly sealed, in the refrigerator, for a very long time.

Cucumber Panzanella with Horseradish & Parsley

A good panzanella relies on a contrast of flavors and textures—and, obviously, a sh*t ton of croutons. Here, it means fresh and crunchy cucumbers alongside tender sweet tomatoes, crunchy nuggets of toasted focaccia and a bracing vinaigrette. I love a really sharp acidic dressing, and this one is no exception: There's a double hit of horseradish and Dijon that soaks into the focaccia.

For the dressing:

3 tablespoons white wine vinegar

2 tablespoons finely grated fresh horseradish, or 1 tablespoon prepared

2 teaspoons Dijon mustard

1 shallot, finely chopped

¼ cup olive oil

Kosher salt and freshly ground black pepper

For the salad:

4 cups cubed day-old focaccia (about 9 ounces)

2 tablespoons olive oil, plus more for drizzling

2 cups parsley leaves

1 pound Persian or other seedless cucumbers (about 6), roughly chopped

1 green or yellow heirloom tomato, roughly chopped

Kosher salt and freshly ground black pepper

serves 4

Make the dressing: In a large bowl, whisk together the vinegar, horseradish, mustard, shallot and oil; season with salt and pepper. Set aside.

Make the salad: Preheat the oven to 400°. Spread the focaccia on a rimmed baking sheet and toss with 2 tablespoons of oil. Bake until golden and toasted, 6 to 8 minutes. Add to the dressing along with the parsley, cucumbers and tomato and toss to combine. Season to taste with salt and pepper. Drizzle with more oil and serve.

Cucumber Sandwiches with Toasted-Hazelnut Cream Cheese

If you've ever been to a high tea (or a low one, for that matter), you've probably encountered a cucumber sandwich. Often built on spongy white bread with a schmear of butter (or, heaven forbid, margarine), the sandwich is only as good as its raw ingredients. I like a sturdier canvas, and although this snack will work on any decent rye bread, these finger sandwiches are especially good on dense squares of Danish rye. If you opt for more of a Jewish deli-style rye, you might want to toast the bread first, but that's your call.

4 ounces cream cheese

½ cup toasted hazelnuts

8 slices dark rye or pumpernickel bread

2 Persian cucumbers, thinly sliced

Kosher salt and freshly ground black pepper

1 lemon, halved

Chopped fresh chives

serves 4

In a food processor, combine the cream cheese and hazelnuts and process to combine (you can leave the nuts as coarsely or smoothly chopped as you like). Spread about 1 tablespoon of hazelnut cream cheese on 1 side of each slice of bread. Top 4 of the cream cheese–smeared sides with a layer of cucumbers, and season with salt and pepper. Squeeze a little lemon juice over the cucumbers and sprinkle with chives. Sandwich with the remaining 4 slices of bread, cream cheese side down. Cut off the crusts (if you like) and cut each sandwich into 4 squares, rectangles or triangles. Arrange the sandwiches on a platter and serve.

Sweet Onion-Cucumber Sandwiches with Mustard Butter

I like to use smaller, thinner Persian cucumbers whenever I add them to sandwiches. Their dainty diameter makes them easy to eat in regular-size bites, so you won't have any awkward sandwich-eating moments. I prefer a couple layers of very thinly sliced cucumber to just one layer of thick slices. The same goes for the sweet onion. If you have a mandoline, use it for this effect.

- 4 tablespoons unsalted butter, at room temperature
- 1 tablespoon whole grain mustard
- 1 tablespoon Dijon mustard
- ¼ teaspoon kosher salt
- 8 slices thin white sandwich bread
- 2 Persian cucumbers, thinly sliced
- 4 very thin slices sweet onion
- Flaky salt and freshly ground black pepper

serves 4

In a small bowl, mash the butter with both mustards and the kosher salt until evenly combined. Spread some of the butter on 1 side of each slice of bread. Top 4 of the buttered sides with the cucumbers and onion and season with flaky salt and several grinds of black pepper. Sandwich with the remaining 4 slices of bread, mustard-butter side down. Cut off the crusts if you like and cut each sandwich into 4 squares, rectangles or triangles. For extra credit, punch out shapes with cookie cutters (circles and stars work best—witches on broomsticks, not so much). Arrange the sandwiches on a platter and serve.

Cucumber & Tomatillo Relish

Oh, snap! This one is good. And it's made almost entirely in the food processor, so it comes together lickety-split. You can use any type of cucumber you want, but keep in mind that as cucumbers get bigger and more mature, their seeds can become bitter. If you're using, for example, half of a large cucumber here, just use a spoon to scoop the seeds out before chopping the flesh. This dip keeps very well, so you can snack on it for days. Pack it on ice and take it to the beach. It's great with corn or pita chips and even more sensational on fish tacos.

8 ounces tomatillos, husks removed, roughly chopped

1 serrano chile, roughly chopped (optional)

Small handful cilantro leaves and tender stems (about ½ cup)

1 medium cucumber (about 8 ounces), chopped to about ¼-inch dice

1 teaspoon kosher salt

1 teaspoon sugar

makes 1½ cups

In a food processor, combine the tomatillos, chile and cilantro and pulse until very finely chopped. Transfer the mixture to a bowl and fold in the cucumber, salt and sugar. The relish will keep, tightly covered, in the refrigerator for about 4 days.

Cucumber Raita with Crispy Lamb & Chickpeas

When I was in 12th grade, my English teacher taught us about a literary foil—a character who contrasts with another to highlight his (usually the protagonist's) particular characteristics—using the example of a string of pearls on a piece of black velvet. When I teach 12th-grade English, I'll explain foils using the example of this dark and crispy spiced lamb against cool and creamy herb and cucumber raita. Same-same, right? Cucumbers are thought to have originated in India, so it's no surprise that their refreshing cooling crunch pairs so well with big flavors of pungent spices, chile and lamb.

For the raita:

2 cups Greek yogurt (preferably full fat)

2 medium cucumbers (about 1 pound)—peeled, seeded and finely chopped

1 tablespoon chopped cilantro

1 tablespoon chopped mint

1 garlic clove, finely grated

½ teaspoon ground cumin

Juice of half a lemon

Kosher salt and freshly ground black pepper

serves 6 to 8

For the lamb and chickpeas:

2 tablespoons neutral oil (such as vegetable)

1 small yellow onion, finely chopped

2 garlic cloves, finely chopped

1 hot chile, such as serrano or jalapeño, finely chopped

8 ounces ground lamb

½ teaspoon garam masala

½ teaspoon ground cumin

½ teaspoon ground coriander

One 15-ounce can chickpeas, rinsed and drained (or 1½ cups cooked chickpeas)

Cilantro leaves and tender stems, for serving

Warm pita bread, for serving

Make the raita: In a large bowl, combine the yogurt, cucumbers, cilantro, mint, garlic, cumin and lemon juice and stir to combine. Season to taste with salt and a little pepper, add more lemon juice if you like and set aside.

Make the lamb and chickpeas: In a large skillet, heat the oil over medium-high heat. Add the onion and garlic and cook, stirring often, until the vegetables are soft and golden, 5 to 7 minutes. Add the chile and lamb and cook, breaking the meat up with a wooden spoon, until cooked through, about 4 minutes.

Add the garam masala, cumin, coriander and chickpeas and stir to combine. Cook, undisturbed, pressing down with the back of the spoon until the mixture is dark and crispy in spots, about 2 minutes. Toss and repeat until mostly crispy throughout, 6 to 8 minutes total.

Spread the raita on a large platter and top with the lamb mixture and cilantro leaves. Serve with warm pita.

Grilled Cucumber Guacamole

When I was in culinary school, one of our rotations included making lunch for the other students. Forever an intimidated line cook, I offered to prep guacamole and set about chopping onions and tomatoes, grating garlic and roasting jalapeños. My friend Michael came over and said, "Uh, Dawn, what are you doing?" "Making guacamole!" I replied, excitable as usual. Michael grew up in a big Mexican family and promptly explained that I was making "dip." "Guacamole is three things," he told me. "Avocados, lime juice, salt...maybe a little cilantro." To this day that's how I make most of my guacamole, but every once in a while I'll try something outside of the *caja*. Give this one a try when you're feeling daring—and when Michael's not looking.

- 2 avocados, halved and pitted
- 1 medium cucumber (about 8 ounces), halved lengthwise
- 1 jalapeño chile
- 1 tablespoon olive oil, plus more for brushing
- Kosher salt
- ½ small onion, finely chopped (about ⅓ cup)
- ¼ cup chopped fresh cilantro
- Juice of 1 lime

makes **2** *cups*

Prepare a grill for medium-high direct heat or preheat a grill pan over medium-high heat. Brush the avocados, cucumber and jalapeño with oil and season with salt. Grill the vegetables, starting cut-side down and turning occasionally, until they're lightly charred, 10 to 12 minutes total. Let cool slightly.

When the cucumber is cool enough to handle, chop it into ¼- to ½-inch dice. Discard the stem from the jalapeño and finely chop (if you want less heat, discard the seeds). Scoop the flesh from the avocados and lightly mash it in a medium bowl. Add the chopped cucumber, jalapeño, onion, cilantro, lime juice and 1 tablespoon of oil. Season really well with salt and gently mix to combine. Serve immediately with tortilla chips or alongside tacos.

Hot Day, Cool Snack

Slice some cucumbers, sprinkle with flaky salt and red pepper flakes (as much as you like) and squeeze a half a lemon or lime over top.

Cucumber & Fruit Salad with Green-Tea Syrup

Cucumbers play nicely with anything sweet-tart, so feel free to tinker with the apple and kiwi, substituting green plums or grapes or nectarines instead. If you happen to find (or be growing) lemon verbena, it would be very nice scattered over the top.

½ cup sugar

1 bag green tea

1 English cucumber, thinly sliced

1 sweet-tart apple such as Granny Smith or Pink Lady, thinly sliced crosswise through the core, seeds removed

2 kiwis, peeled and sliced crosswise

serves 4 *to* 6

In a small saucepan, combine the sugar and ½ cup of water. Bring to a boil and cook, swirling occasionally, until the sugar has dissolved, about 4 minutes. Remove the pan from the heat and add the green tea bag. Set the tea aside to steep for about 10 minutes. Remove the tea bag, squeezing to extract as much tea flavor as possible, and let the syrup cool completely.

In a large bowl, combine the cucumber, apple and kiwi. Pour the syrup over the top and toss the mixture gently to combine. Refrigerate the salad for at least 30 minutes and up to 1 day before serving.

Cucumber & Honeydew Paletas

Ice-pop molds are one of those things most of us had in the house when we were kids but never end up with as grown-ups...until we have kids. Kids or no kids, do yourself a favor and get a set so you can make these paletas. If you can't find molds, or don't want to buy them, you can freeze these paletas in little Mason jars or Dixie cups.

1 medium seedless cucumber (about 8 ounces), peeled and chopped

1 cup cubed honeydew melon

1 to 2 tablespoons sugar (depending on your sweetness preference)

2 tablespoons fresh lime juice

1 jalapeño chile, seeds removed for less heat (optional)

Pinch kosher salt

makes **8**

In a blender, combine the cucumber, honeydew, sugar, lime juice, jalapeño (if using) and salt and puree until smooth. Transfer to eight 2-ounce ice-pop molds, insert popsicle sticks in them and freeze until firm, at least 4 hours and up to 24. Remove the pops from the molds (you can run the molds under cool water briefly to help unmold the pops) and serve, or place in a ziptop bag and return to the freezer for up to 2 weeks.

Thank You!

Thanks to all of those who happily ate mostly cucumbers for about six weeks straight. Thanks to my family for teaching me to eat and making cucumbers part of the regular rotation. Thanks to my food friends for keeping me sharp and challenging me to do better. Thanks to the Short Stack team for making it easy. And thanks to Matt for every big and little thing.

—Dawn Perry

Share your Short Stack cooking experiences with us
(or just keep in touch) via:

#shortstackeds
@shortstackeds
facebook.com/shortstackeditions
hello@shortstackeditions.com

Colophon

This edition of Short Stack was printed by Stephen Gould Corp. in Richmond, Virginia on Neenah Astrobrights Vulcan Green (interior) and Neenah Oxford White (cover) paper. The main text of the book is set in Futura and Jensen Pro, and the headlines are set in Lobster.

Available now at ShortStackEditions.com:

Vol. 1 | Eggs,
by Ian Knauer

Vol. 2 | Tomatoes,
by Soa Davies

Vol. 3 | Strawberries,
by Susan Spungen

Vol. 4 | Buttermilk,
by Angie Mosier

Vol. 5 | Grits,
by Virginia Willis

Vol. 6 | Sweet Potatoes,
by Scott Hocker

Vol. 7 | Broccoli,
by Tyler Kord

Vol. 8 | Honey,
by Rebekah Peppler

Vol. 9 | Plums,
by Martha Holmberg

Vol. 10 | Corn,
by Jessica Battilana

Vol. 11 | Apples,
by Andrea Albin

Vol. 12 | Brown Sugar,
by Libbie Summers

Vol. 13 | Lemons,
by Alison Roman

Vol. 14 | Prosciutto di Parma,
by Sara Jenkins

Vol. 15 | Summer Squash,
by Sarah Baird

Vol. 16 | Peaches,
by Beth Lipton

Vol. 17 | Chickpeas,
by Victoria Granof

Vol. 18 | Chocolate,
by Susie Heller

Vol. 19 | Maple Syrup,
by Casey Elsass

Vol. 20 | Rhubarb,
by Sheri Castle

Vol. 21 | Cherries,
by Stacy Adimando

Vol. 22 | Eggplant,
by Raquel Pelzel

Vol. 23 | Tahini,
by Adeena Sussman

Vol. 24 | Ginger,
by Mindy Fox

Vol. 25 | Avocados,
by Katie Quinn

Vol. 26 | Peanuts,
by Steven Satterfield

Vol. 27 | Coconut,
by Ben Mims

Vol. 28 | Cucumbers,
by Dawn Perry